THE GRIFFIN POETRY PRIZE
Anthology 2015

Published in Canada in 2015 and in the USA in 2015 by House of Anansi Press Inc.

House of Anansi Press
110 Spadina Avenue, Suite 801
Toronto, ON, M5V 2K4
Tel. 416-363-4343
Fax 416-363-1017
www.houseofanansi.com

House of Anansi Press is committed to protecting our natural environment. As part of our
efforts, the interior of this book is printed on paper made from second-growth forests and is
acid-free.

19 18 17 16 15   1 2 3 4 5

Library and Archives Canada Cataloguing in Publication

Cataloguing data available from Library and Archives Canada

Cover design: Chloé Griffin and Kyra Griffin
Cover image: Chloé Griffin
Photograph on inside front and back cover: Chloé Griffin
Typesetting: Marijke Friesen

Canada Council Conseil des Arts
for the Arts du Canada

ONTARIO ARTS COUNCIL
CONSEIL DES ARTS DE L'ONTARIO
an Ontario government agency
un organisme du gouvernement de l'Ontario

*We acknowledge for their financial support of our publishing program
the Canada Council for the Arts, the Ontario Arts Council, and the Government of Canada
through the Canada Book Fund.*

Printed and bound in Canada

THE GRIFFIN POETRY PRIZE

Anthology 2015

A SELECTION OF THE SHORTLIST

Edited by TIM BOWLING

2001
Paul Celan (International)
Translated by Heather
McHugh and Nikolai Popov
Anne Carson (Canadian)

2002
Alice Notley (International)
Christian Bök (Canadian)

2003
Paul Muldoon (International)
Margaret Avison (Canadian)

2004
August Kleinzahler
    (International)
Anne Simpson (Canadian)

2005
Charles Simic (International)
Roo Borson (Canadian)

2006
Kamau Brathwaite
    (International)
Sylvia Legris (Canadian)

2007
Charles Wright (International)
Don McKay (Canadian)

2008
John Ashbery (International)
Robin Blaser (Canadian)

2009
C. D. Wright (International)
A. F. Moritz (Canadian)

2010
Eiléan Ní Chuillieanáin
    (International)
Karen Solie (Canadian)

2011
Gjertrud Schnackenberg
    (International)
Dionne Brand (Canadian)

2012
David Harsent (International)
Ken Babstock (Canadian)

2013
Ghassan Zaqtan (International)
Translated by Fady Joudah
David W. McFadden
    (Canadian)

2014
Brenda Hillman (International)
Anne Carson (Canadian)

CONTENTS

PREFACE

The smell of fresh coffee, the sound of my children's voices, and the sight of another stack of books to read and assess for the Griffin International Poetry Prize. Every day, from early November to late February, this holy trinity of sensory experience defined my life. And if you're thinking, "Well, that's a pretty nice life," I agree with you 100%. Or, rather, only 92%. I must reserve a small percentage for those days when the poetry was unremarkable, lacking linguistic energy and engaging content, and for when the very heavy burden of my responsibility as one of three judges (along with Fanny Howe and Piotr Sommer) for such a prestigious and financially rewarding honour as the Griffin Prize forced me to assess and re-assess my assessments.

As the process neared its completion, and the 560 entries turned into longlists of twenty books, and then shorter longlists of six to eight books, and then, finally, the official shortlists and winners, I began to experience sleepless nights. As someone raised in a working-class family by two people raised in poverty during the Great Depression, I realized all-too-keenly just how much money was at stake along with the considerable recognition. Poets, of course, must live in the "real" world as well as in their imaginations, and the money attached to the Griffin Prize purchases that most precious of tools in the poet's tool kit: time.

Then the question became: how much time for this jury work was *enough* time? I could hear the 560 poets asking for one more read, and so I would often return to the books and engage with the voices all over again. Did I eventually tire of the great harvest

I myself desired? Not quite. But it was no easy task, at the end of those four intense months, to leave excellence off the shortlists in favour of …well …a higher degree of excellence.

Ultimately, and happily, that is how the whole process ended — with seven excellent poets being recognized for their hard work and commitment to their craft and vision. What defines the poems of all the shortlisted poets is the sense of urgency pushing the lines, the realization on the reader's part that these poems had to be written, that they were composed out of an inner compulsion that, in the powerful way of poetry, translates the highly individual voice into a communal pleasure. These seven poets have something vital to say and the skill to say it memorably — the proof is here on these pages and in the pages of their individual volumes.

And what has become of my holy trinity? I have the coffee still, and my children's voices, but the jury work for the Griffin Prize is over. All that remains now is the gala evening (what did Groucho Marx say? I'd love a gala evening, but at my age, I can't keep up that pace).

No, that is not all that remains. There is, of course, the work and the pleasure of poetry — the reading and the writing of it — that goes on as long as there's breath in the body. I'm always happy to return there, to what George Mackay Brown calls the poet's "true task: interrogation of silence."

But before I take my leave, I wish to thank my fellow jurors, Ruth Smith of the Griffin Trust, and Scott Griffin and the trustees of the Griffin Trust, for the gift of those four months, and for the chance to celebrate not only these fine poets represented here, but poetry itself. More than a responsibility, it has been an immense privilege.

Tim Bowling, April 2015

INTERNATIONAL
SHORTLIST

WANG XIAONI

ELEANOR GOODMAN

Something Crosses My Mind

What is so attractive about Wang Xiaoni's poems as translated into English by Eleanor Goodman is her quiet, loving, meditative distance to the mostly anonymous and lonely heroes she clearly knows well. And her attitude to time, which she keeps dragging out of its anchored localities (and barely marked history) to extend and connect, or fuse with specific spaces that she also enlarges in size and scope. Moments prolong into a century or a life, imaginary beasts meld with real animals, description becomes an act of meditation. In a few lines, a village can take on the dimension of a vast landscape — and yet still remain that particular village. And while Xiaoni's characters may not speak, they seem to have a real insight into our experience and lives. In a way nothing much happens in her magic lyricism: the wind blows, the ocean rises, people work or move from one place to another, or wait, or just leave some place, and they have souls (which behave like shadows). Reading her, I found myself repeating Auden's phrase "About suffering they were never wrong, / The old Masters." Wang Xiaoni is a terrific contemporary poet gracefully extending the great classical Chinese tradition.

The Watermelon's Sorrow

After I've paid
the watermelon comes along like a blindfolded prisoner.

We get on the bus
this guy who's never changed his coat in his life
with no bones but too much blood
who grew up being thumped countless times.

Halfway there I take a turn
there's always something to keep us from home.
The watermelon with its artificially extended life
hits painfully off the sides of the bus.
It's as hard to want to die as it is to want to live
nightlights illuminate a closing knife shop.
The watermelon comes with me
it can only go farther and farther away
I'll use all my hands to steady its
big blood-filled head.

Without rhyme or reason, I carry the melon along
and without rhyme or reason, my busyness carries me.

Seeing the Ocean from a Night Flight

Everything becomes small
only the ocean makes the night's leather clothes
open up the further out it spreads.

Flying north
to the right is Tianjin
to the left is Beijing
two clusters of moths flinging themselves at fire.

Then the East China Sea suddenly moves
the wind brings silver bits that can't be more shattered
and many thick wrinkles whip up

I see the face of the ocean
I see the aged seashore
trembling and hugging the world too tightly.

I have seen death
but never seen death come back to life like that.

Plowman

He is turning over the whole mountaintop with a plow.

He follows behind an ox
and the two reveal the earth's forehead by force.
A dark red wound appears
the red seen after a fever passes.
The red that comes after punishment.
The red that comes after pain has been quietly survived.

Suddenly the small plowman disappears
the just-turned red mud has buried him in the mountainside.
His partner raises his enormous head
like he's another plowman wearing an ox mask
like the pair at the front and back of the plow are brothers.

The tobacco seeds are still in the burlap sack
the work has just begun.
They stop
one coughing high the other low
then dust covers their faces, and everything is quiet again.

Wheat Seedlings

On the mountainside field after field of wheat seedlings shiver
the farther up the more they tremble
the mountain will soon shake itself apart.

Spring borrows the wind
to spread a fear of heights even farther.
It seems a transparent weapon is hidden in the heart of the sky
it seems danger wants to drop down and stab us.

There is a bundle of light walking about
the sun is preparing to make the green even greener.
The wheat seedlings ooze bile in fear
one by one the mountaintops connect, light up.

The wheat keeps spreading into the pitch-black towns
the bread steamed on the fire breaks open.
Those who have eaten their fill go outside
to turn up a roiling red clay tail.
The red tail's human leader also strolls up to the mountaintop
the only thing on earth that seems timid is the wheat.

The green color's fear is of the hoe.
It's of the piercing bright blade of the sickle.
And it's of us, the flour-eaters.

At the Village Fair

A gray overcast fair
a half-day panting sluggish fair.
Two motorcycles are filling up their tanks
a pig is trussed up in the middle of the street
the knife-sharpener wipes sweat from his nose.

Who'd have thought the pig would escape in a blink
shiny and black, it fled fast.

It's fine to lose some things, but not the pig.
The knife-grabbers, the bicycle-riders, the ones carrying scales
the whole village gave chase,
a streetful of black-clad galloping animals.

The pig's escape was the high point of the day
as he ditched this inescapable old town.
The flagstone streets showed their smooth junctures
layer after layer of crow-colored tiles
the morning turned bright
outside in a cracked mud pot, cacti competed to bloom purple
    flowers.

And so the fair became a utopia
thanks to the one who declared war, thanks to those who didn't
    submit.

At Night What's Inside the Skyscrapers

There need not be people, but there can't not be electricity.
Electricity sends the steps up
and sends the light up
sends neon into the sky.

People built a skyscraper
they hurried to put in electricity and then withdrew.
Let it stand alone at the darkest battlefront
forehead poisonously bright
like an able-bodied man, like an idiot
like a self-proclaimed hero.
Its whole body covered in sparkling metals, its whole body hiding
    explosives
its whole body leaking blood toward the sky.

And now I expose the ironed sheets
I put out all the lights.
The skyscrapers are unbearably bright
I take an eye-closing pill.
In this life to be human is already glorious.

The One Sticking Close to the White Wall as He Leaves

He sticks close to himself as he leaves.
His soul follows close behind, appearing on the wall.

He doesn't notice the separation at all
doesn't care about that old thing
he leaves it all on its own.
The soul meets a fly, the fly escapes
it encounters graffiti on the wall, the filthy words leap and dodge.

Caring only for himself he hurries on, sticking to the wretched
    graying wall.
In front is himself
behind is the hovering soul
twisting and turning to follow close
as though terrified to lose its way
that poor helpless little orphan.

If he walks a little faster
he might lose that anxious tail.
Even faster
and the wall won't have anything to do with the passersby
just one large swath of good winter sunlight.

WIOLETTA GREG

MAREK KAZMIERSKI

Finite Formulae & Theories of Chance

These poems, as translated from Polish into English by Marek Kazmierski, retain the force of first experience and, equally, a collection of history's remains. Greg's thoughts include the catastrophe of the 20th century whose marks still wobble before her eyes, and into the experience of living in post-Communist Poland. This stunning collection shows us (mostly through the eyes and memories of childhood) a world of objects transported across years. "Tossing satin bulbs into wicker baskets," the child poet is at ease with the earth and the hardy objects made from it. Greg grants us the privilege of seeing what she saw before she saw more.

Half-Term

Sliding down our frozen hill
on sacks stuffed full of hay,
we swallow clumps of air, pieces
of sky, slaloming border posts.
I empty my moon-boots of icy shards,
my soaked gloves stiffening,
and again run up the mound as if entranced,
hoping all of half-term will be like this.

My Mont Blanc is melting with all this friction.
The sun fading faster than adrenaline
from our flaming cheeks.
Torches come peering through bushes.
Someone shouts: – Go home! – so we go.
Eyes freezing over like tiny planets.

Smena's Memory

She left me with two pictures and the suspicion
that something other than blood lines binds us.
Maybe a tendency to give rise to quick feelings,
quivers she captured with a Soviet-made camera.

Her hair turned darker after her First Communion.
The wristwatch she received as a gift squeaked.
A wee spring broke. Time racing
past her first period. A painful
childhood which did not heal with time.

At thirty, she began to wake.
Like an old turtle dove warming
an empty nest out of sheer habit,
in a council flat she learnt
how to swear, iron shirts for the one
who peels potatoes without being asked.

– Can the finite ever go on too long?

Spring, 1986

The night was heavy, but the air was alive.

MIKE OLDFIELD

At night, the Chernobyl cloud fell
across pastures. Thyroids swelled.
The pond glowed with murmuring iodine,
swallows kissing crooked mirrors.

The radio kept playing "Moonlight Shadow".
In the barn, a girl guide from the city started
a club for virgins. Smoking menthols,
we took lessons in preparing for conjugal
life from copies of *Playboy* instead.

There would be no other end to the world,
and yet it kept coming, like cramps
and acne, until I discovered
spots of dark blood in my underwear.

Stargate

A white night. Lime crumbling away from the bark of the old
    apple tree
which blocks our view of the house. Again, we choose to sleep
    outside.

Two muskrats crawl out of the pond. Their wet hides,
like torn tinsel, holding strange fires captive.

I lie inside an empty gutter as if it were the pearly gates,
while you slip between my lips a boiled sweet.

Pips

I enter the paper mill with a basket of cherries.
The steel gate bears sulphur etchings,
banners holding up our nation's future.
The country stumbles over woodchip tiling,
holding reams of paper, still warm,
which will only reach full maturity in an office.

Night shifts crawl from intercity coaches,
stamping their dates on time sheets.
Father smoking at the reception desk,
his hands shaking over the console
as he remotes the gates open and shut.

Ever since the day I discovered
that both of us are mortal,
nothing's passed between us but time.

A Wedding Party

Our family traipses home at dawn,
through fields of poppies
the police haven't sniffed out yet.

Children, their tiny boots knocking
the heads off bluish puff-balls,
fighting off mists with a flagging balloon.

We walk as exhausted as nun moths
which, having copulated all night,
rest on a bed of oak leaves.

Damp air turning talc solid
in wrinkles, unfurling perms,
seeking a higher incarnation
in far-off lights.

Someone's slip-on shoe in a steaming turd,
puke on a clump of horseradish leaves.

We struggle across boggy meadows,
stumbling through the Valley of Josaphat.

MICHAEL LONGLEY

The Stairwell

Part of the excitement and pleasure of Michael Longley's *The Stairwell* comes from the quiet unpredictability of what his language does. It is modest and unassuming, yet bold in its deceptively small meditations. His sentences achieve their goals through sophisticatedly simple means: Longley loves to understate (or underplay), retard (and see how far he can go), imply, question, and enumerate (long enumeration in short poems is part of his signature). This book, including the elegy sequence that comprises the whole second section, is a masterly realization of the light touch he brings to serious subjects, as if sentences were his way of breathing. And they do not behave conventionally, despite his life-long study of such basic things as love, friendship, death, experience, memory, historical memory included, and of some other disciplines that go along with them, like learning to know nature for instance. There's also a lot to learn from Michael Longley — part of the pleasure is the detailed knowledge and wisdom the poems bring. While greatly attached to certain classical rules, Longley has always paid homage to them so interestingly, simultaneously mastering and subverting them. *The Stairwell* is a book by a major poet writing at the height of his powers.

The Stairwell

for Lucy McDiarmid

I have been thinking about the music for my funeral –
Liszt's transcription of that Schumann song, for instance,
'Dedication' – inwardness meets the poetry of excess –
When you lead me out of your apartment to demonstrate
In the Halloween-decorated lobby the perfect acoustic
Of the stairwell, and stand among pumpkins, cobwebby
Skulls, dancing skeletons, and blow kisses at the ceiling,
Whistling Great War numbers – 'Over There', 'It's a Long,
Long Way', 'Keep the Home Fires Burning' (the refrain) –
As though for my father who could also whistle them,
Trench memories, your eyes closed, your head tilted back,
Your cheeks filling up with air and melody and laughter.
I hold the banister. I touch your arm. Listen, Lucy,
There are songbirds circling high up in the stairwell.

Notebook

I

Why did I never keep a notebook
That filled up with reed buntings
And blackcaps and chiffchaffs, their
Songs a subsong between the lines?

Early April. I am seventeen.
Under an overhanging whin bush
I have spotted linnets building.
A robin has laid her first egg.

II

I find dead on her nest
A lapwing, beneath her
Three perfect eggs, and one
Without shell or colour
That bursts when I touch it.

Her mate sky-suspended
Screaming around my head
Swoops as though to blind me
When I take her in my hands
And look at her torn hole.

III

Who was the professor who took me
Mackerel-fishing off Killard Point?
A marine biologist, he taught me
To brain fish against the gunwales.

On the raised beach I picked out
From pebbles a plover's egg:
It cracked in my trouser pocket
Like a chilly ejaculation.

Amelia's Poem

Amelia, your newborn name
Combines with the midwife's word
And, like smoke from driftwood fires,
Wafts over the lochside road
Past the wattle byre – hay bales
For ponies, Silver and Whisper –
Between drystone walls' river-
Rounded moss-clad ferny stones,
Through the fenceless gate and gorse
To the flat erratic boulder
Where otters and your mother rest,
Spraints black as your *meconium*,
Fish bones, fish scales, shitty sequins
Reflecting what light remains.

Marigolds, 1960

You are dying. Why do we fight?
You find my first published poem –
'Not worth the paper it's printed on,'
You say. *She gave him marigolds –*

You are dying. 'They've cut out my
Wheesht – I have to sit down
To *wheesht* – like a woman' –
Marigolds *the colour of autumn.*

I need to hitchhike to Dublin
For Trinity Term. 'I'll take you
Part of the way,' you say,
'And we can talk if you like.'

And we talk and talk as though
We know we are just in time.
'A little bit further,' you say
Again and again, and in pain.

A few miles from Drogheda
You turn the car. We say goodbye
And you drive away slowly
Towards Belfast and your death.

To keep in his cold room. Look
At me now on the Newry Road
Standing beside my rucksack. Och,
Daddy, look in your driving mirror.

Boat

for Seamus

What's the Greek for boat,
You ask, old friend,
Fellow voyager
Approaching Ithaca –
Oh, flatulent sails,
Wave-winnowing oars,
Shingle-scrunching keel –
But, so close to home,
There's a danger always
Of amnesiac storms,
Waterlogged words.

19 July 2011

Psalm

One wreath had blackberry clusters
Intertwined. Was it a blackbird
Or wren that briefly sang a graveside
Aria, godlike in its way, a psalm?
(He will defend you under his wing.
You will be safe under his feathers.)

5 October 2013

Hailstones

at the Memorial to the Murdered Jews of Europe, Berlin

It must have been God or, rather, Yahweh
Who scattered the granite slabs with hailstones
And threw them from His hand so accurately
Not one Jew was uncommemorated.

The Wheelchair

Pushing you in your wheelchair to the sea
I look down at your yellowy bald patch
And recall your double-crown's tufty hair.

You were the naughtier twin, were you not?
It was I who wept when you were chastised.
Where am I pushing you, dear brother, where?

The Mule-Cart

An engineer, you would appreciate
The technique for yoking the mule-cart –
When they fasten a wicker basket on top
And take down from its peg a boxwood yoke
With knob and guide-hooks for holding the reins
And bring out the lashing-rope – fourteen feet long –
And settle the yoke on the well-polished pole
And slip the eye of the rope over a peg
And tie the rope three times around the knob
And secure it all the way down the pole
And twist it under a hook and thus yoke
Strong-footed draught-mules to the mule-cart.
(What's the function of the peg exactly?)

SPENCER REECE

The Road to Emmaus

This is an open book, a welcoming one like a voice on the phone we instantly remember. Maybe Frank O'Hara has returned? Maybe the Berrigans, including Ted? What happiness to hear that good-natured tone again! Spencer Reece has slipped in among us, without any forewarning or embarrassment, his poems like faces turning to call us to follow them. Who is he? Let's go. Whether he knew it or not, the experience of reading his poems is similar to the recognition moment on the road to Emmaus. We are glad to trust so completely. In these poems we also meet a kind of "innocent American" in the best, almost lost sense.

1 Corinthians 13

How long do we wait for love?
Long ago, we rowed on a pond.
Our oars left the moon broken—
our gestures ruining the surface.
Our parents wanted us to marry.
Beyond the roses where we lay,
men who loved men grew wounds.
When do we start to forget our age?
Your husband and I look the same.
All day, your mother confuses us
as her dementia grows stronger.
Your boys yell: *Red Rover!*
We whisper your sister's name
like librarians; at last on the list,
her heart clapping in her rib cage,
having stopped now six times,
the pumps opened by balloons,
we await her new heart cut
out from the chest of a stranger.
Your old house settles in its bones,
pleased by how we are arranged.
Our shadow grows like an obituary.
One of us says: "It is getting so dark."
Your children end their game.
Trees stiffen into scrapbooks.
The sky's shelves fill with stars.

The Prodigal Son

"Fly at once!" he said. "All is discovered." — Edward Gorey

For A. J. Verdelle

In Miami, this May afternoon, I look up,
the sky hot, so hot, always, and heating up hotter—
how long I have loved this scene.
The clouds are white optimistic churches;
I cannot number them.
Herons, pelicans, and gulls glide like dreams
through cloud portals, cloud porticos, and cloud porte cocheres
Giotto could have done
with his passion for blues and dimensions.
Hard not to love a place always called by possibility.
Nearby, Cuba is singing and somewhere here
Richard Blanco is writing his poems.
As I enter the city,
my bishop walks with a cane towards our cathedral.

The sun shines on the people
and unites us in a delirium of light.
High above this bleached, scorched, fragile, groin-scented
    peninsula,
birds track their insects and remain loyal to their nests.
I look up and I feel bliss building
as I did when my father read another book to me,
and another, the pages like wings.
There are moments of memorable patience in this world.
Airplanes advance towards Miami International,
carrying Jewish retirees and Cuban émigrés—
their descending engines disrupt the white-gloved illegal waiters
at the country clubs in Coral Gables, who deliver flan
to ladies who have pulled skin behind their ears like gum.

This is a place where few decisions are doubted.
On South Beach,
where everyone rearranges or expands their sexual parts,
there seems to be no life outside the physical and time
becomes a tricky thing here, spring looks like winter,
winter like spring, the scenes dense, shifting, shut—
and before you know it the rats have preached from the mangoes
and then chewed them into corpses.
And look how the interior decorators
unroll their fresh bolts and wink-wink to new clients—
what would be considered frivolous anywhere else
is here pondered and coerced at great length.
The feminine gains strength.

Moving closer to the cathedral,
the sea presses the harbor, wanting to be loved,
pushing up the cruise ships with its muscles.
The sea says: "I am the sea."
We have seen Cubans arrive atop dolphins' backs here.
Mothers have drowned for their sons,
but the cool gray backs of the dolphins have buoyed their children
     to us,
numbed by the lullaby of sonar clicks.
The sea blesses the city the way mothers do—
forceful, pushy, ungraspable, persistent.
Black mangrove shoots take root on the porous chalky rock,
building themselves up like steeples. Listen.
How the waves love what does not love them back.

Pedicurists buff the toenails of the sugar daddies in the Delano.
Lincoln Road refines its scarlet seductions.
Bees are sticky with tourism inside the motel rooms of the rose.
Red-orange petals from the Royal Poincianas tint the minutes
with flamboyance. Fuchsia bottlebrush blossoms
explode with seeds. I will always love my time in this city,

you might say craziest of cities,
delivering its youth in short shorts
and Rollerblades with rainbow sweatbands.

City smelling of unzipped things.
I do not think the city will ever be mine.
Beautiful Spanish and broken English spoken everywhere.
How I love that sound,
for it is the sound of people making their way
where they were not born.
Maids from Honduras push their carts,
stacking their wrapped soaps,
their cuticles sting with disinfectant,
perspiration staining their uniforms.

O Miami!
For a decade I did not speak to my parents.
Are you listening to me?
I will not bore you with details.
Instead, I will tell you something new.
Listen to me. I was angry.
But the reasons no longer interest me.
I take the liberty of assuming you approve of forgiveness,
stressing hardening gentleness as you do.
I speak to my bishop about my call and the sacraments,
we discuss absolutions, blessings, consecrations—
our work of the soul. The soul has no sex and I am relieved
to speak of a thing alive in the world that has no sex.

The bishop places a paperweight atop my reports on his desk,
our professional talk is measured by the silence of the dead
who are always flinging open their shutters,
religion being the work of the living and the dead,
the hope and release of children turning to their parents—
all that business in life that remains unrehearsed.

Superior to obedient, we pray.
The laughter of the bathers
through the grillwork of the office window pleases me,
their movements rinsed in the baptism of the sea, the
    languorous sea.

The sky at the end of the city trembles.
Light and dust warm to cream to pink to lavender.
Miami, it has been a gorgeous day, indeed. Thank you.
How I love your decks, bridges, promenades, and balconies—
the paraphernalia of connection.
How fast the pastels encroach upon the edges.
I have a dinner engagement in Coral Gables at Books & Books
where I will see the poet Richard Blanco.
I hope he will tell me stories of his beloved, broken Cuba.
Nearly five o'clock now, and I am late.
When I arrive, Richard Blanco speaks of Cuba
as I had wished, and the city quiets all around him.
I think, If our bodies house our souls, Richard,
then poets are the interior decorators of the mind.
Richard Blanco is saying something about going back,
his relatives *singing* poems in the fields. I listen.
Nearby, in the palmatum,
at the Fairchild Tropical Botanic Garden,
the Elephant, Date, Malaysian, Kiwi, Coconut, and Royal palms
ask the city to remember their names with the insistence of priests.

Goodbye, Miami, goodbye.
Goodbye to the workers laying down the grids of the concrete
    embeds
on the high-rises, reinforcing their masculine nests,
gluing glass with their spermy compounds to stone and steel.
Goodbye to you, South Beach.
Let your rapturous sands darken to a deep grape color.
Let the polished feet of youth launch into their surprises and swaps.

Let the elements cool.
Goodbye, Richard Blanco, goodbye.
Today my candidacy for Holy Orders was affirmed.
I listen to the sea flatten.
Cuba pleads in the distance one more night.
Honduras waits on too many things to count.
I can stand still no longer.
Stars smooth the sea with their immaculate highways of long lights.

Mother and father,
forgive me my absence.
I will always be moving quietly towards you.

A Few Tender Minutes

It is a summer of rain and I am a seminarian. I visit the Osborn State Correctional Facility. The metal gate opens, then closes behind me, like legs uncrossed and crossed. On the mental health ward, behind a small meshed window, a naked man, wrapped in a bedsheet, poses like Constantine crossing the Milvian Bridge. There is a particular sound in prisons. More insistent than rain, it is the honeyed sound of the hive, the sound of men packed in on top of each other, the sound of regret, anger, and resignation, all beginning and beginning again. I hear them hum in their cells, sticky, strong from barbells. Then I see them—their skins colored black, brown, mocha, plum, peach, and white. Intricate tattoos cover the men like road maps. Semen sweetens the air. A muscular inmate's biceps rise from his T-shirt like loaves of bread. His one-armed boyfriend smokes a cigarette with his hook. We enter the chapel. My fellow seminarian panics. A nurse rushes him to her office in a wheelchair.

We are told the sedated seminarian will not return. Rain messes up Connecticut. Rivers break. Gardens drown. Water collects in the spokes of the spider's web, straightjacketing the flies. In the prison yard, beyond the chain-link fence with razor strips, the landscape runs like a finger painting done by a child. In the thickets, the shadowy traffic of birds in panic. The Carolina wrens have returned to the chokecherry trees— voluble, curious evangelists. The males construct nests with feathers, mud, and twigs. The females inspect and throw out their sticks and sing: "Begin! Begin again!" The male will sing 250 repetitions until a nest can be settled upon. Through the window bars, rain hammers the wrens as they argue over feckless nests.

The clock is a wheelchair disappearing down the corridor of time. We pray with the inmates in a circle. Allowed a few minutes with each inmate, I have time for two. A sex offender says he has been wrongly accused. How will he return to his mother's house? How to begin again? The guard says, "Next." Before me is a man who does not disclose his crime, a Native American who will be released tomorrow. Something about his expression is reminiscent of Sitting Bull after he won the Battle of Little Bighorn and had entered those rodeo shows with Wild Bill to tour Europe: triumphant resignation begins to describe it, but not completely. For forty years, he tells me, his job has been to greet new inmates, which gave him money for toothpaste and pencils. Behind him, a mural of crude voluptuous angels covers the cinder blocks: their wings and breasts have absorbed the Clorox stink of the place. What prayer is in my book for him? The guard picks at his nail beds with his key. He says: "Two more minutes." My crucifix dangles from my chest like a fledgling.

The Poor

By Roberto Sosa, a translation

The poor are many
and so—
impossible to forget.

No doubt,
as day breaks,
they see the buildings
where they wish
they could live with their children.

They
can steady the coffin
of a constellation on their shoulders.
They can wreck
the air like furious birds,
blocking the sun.

But not knowing these gifts,
they enter and exit through mirrors of blood,
walking and dying slowly.

And so,
one cannot forget them.

CANADIAN
SHORTLIST

SHANE BOOK

Congotronic

Here is a contemporary world music that whirls the reader into the centre of the action at once. Here is a spread of thoughts with a winning beat, a door held open to varieties of sound and content from multiple cultures. In these beautifully adept pages, English as we know it is not the only language we are reading but a spread of voices receptive to webs and forms from everywhere else. It's a new poetics but also wholly recognizable in its content. An outcry written to be heard while reading: this poetry signals a breakthrough necessary, innovative, and emotionally piercing.

Security of the First World

This place I have not been.
But alone. Other
possibilities perhaps
and even if I am
of two sliding partitions:
the trees' spacing, tidal
flats punctured by tubular
posts, children—I cannot
arrive at such days,

a fly bumping glass.
Faces may take me
to a station to pick out
hands from stacks of hands.
I continue meaning work
on the metal up into
palatial sound, bricking
a total music of the past.

Water, yes. Include
the hacking text as an excellent
first step, and a flying
picture slashing in ether
flashing a short-lived
shadow. In fact she worked
every day, wedged
between moments of thinking

new cities and a glass bird
furred in monosyllables
no one had bothered
to adopt. She did not
die. A truck came
collecting things and climbing
into the back she entered
a crushingly red sea.

Janelas

I have a home in my son's hand.
The pier is out, the quay closed at noon.
You can sob, so be it, as if dates, as
though you had an oven of dough
everyone wanted. Day, I'm a over it;
out rowing an O.K. used pear,
sailing your barcode, you shop with the pain
you're out now, avowing.
Our row cake vice squeezing through
sewer hour, I sail mystery O
sewer! Made on that pall of rat veil
A forms a dream navy
in the unclear I don't miss saying.

They Cannot Be Taken to Bits

His manhandle was ever "Bat and Toe."
This freedom, he thought, is what makes
his subliminal feel relationship to it
profound, a farther land ever-shimmering.
From somewhere nearby, core odor
of day lily. He set off in pursuit. He kept
a trio of daggers under his dirndl
for just such emergencies.

They Have a Private Career

His boots were broken. When he walked
they said, "Cold only rawed ideas."
He had been at the Colony for many years.
He had been busy culling spores
from the frothy air as the para-mechanical
cloud test come in low over the valley.
Into the late air as into a darkened,
humid dirt basement, he yelled
"Where Tos?" and, "You OKs?"
until the distance became unbearable.

Flagelliform 61: Tilted Away

1

I broke off the dangling shrub   and inserted it   above my ear.
Bent in at the belly   I sweated,   to fit   to try to fit.

2

The dangling shrub   was bruised.
It moved a little move   and Lady Song-of-Jamestown
said in my hear: Why   is broken.

3

Spooked   I
leapt   a leafy thwart
into my thinking vessel   the aluminum canoe
and in my here said Lady Song-of-Jamestown:
"Why   its smelters long ago felled at The-Task-Is-
    Incomplete,   a falling
artist felling them   name of
The-Coriander-of-Mother-and-Child
who wears   crown of shells   partly concealing
a turban of layered light."

4

I stared straight ahead,   paddling.
My canoe walls hung with barkcloth   a giant dentalium
and four figureheads in lignified paste   (We watching).

The ivory one called,   Tapping-Out-of-Time.
And the dark muscular one,   Below-the-Galleon-Decks.
And the remembered one named,   Palm-Thatch-Floor.
And the little one called,   Fruit-of-the-Distant-Weep
    (mothered black,   from sleeping).

5
Lady Song-of-Jamestown   mending her fishnets
pulled the water-hook   from my hand.

6
"Lady Song-of-Jamestown, what shovels you?" I shouted
over my shoulder   and turning
struck her   with my net handle
and broke off the deep brown arm   of   Below-The-
     Galleon-Decks
and drug and drug . . .

7
When at last I got to farthest other shore
I turned to Fruit-of-the-Distant-Weep   saying,
"O chile   for what you sleeping?   Look
at the ripe groceries on the overhanging branch,"   and grabbing
my gray-spined spear   reached up
to tap a bag in the cluster of bags
into the canoe   and with my blade,   halfed it:
toast   mollusky iron telescope pipes   and the posted reward.

8
And though silence descended on Tapping-Out-of-Time
and Palm-Thatch-Floor reeled in some distance,
the Wept-Slept chile   flew open and smiled
scooped up fondles of sea moss   and threw at my feet.

9
And inching along the gunwales
I danced   and danced   "The pushed walk."

Flagelliform 21: Exile ("To Be Sure, Hot Water Kills a Man, but Cold Water Too Kills a Man.")

Mama said for safety we wander.

I remember different lands.

One where soldiers showed me
where all's future war,
war signs tow and end,
shined higher. That's the word: knack.
In the lands we traveled
they give me 'war knack,'
a dunk leer to target the target,
an inner spring sword motor.

One land I learned to track without phone.
Put a notch in a lion.
I learned *serum full a fool that's larger*:
how to wield bladed
phrases, bang
the proverb stick.

Higher abhorred words weirdly near inured
me from getting bashed, an "um"
so dense shimmer designed
could brain the louchest tête.

Another place the General show me
wires for leering, den rug nerve potions,
ant-ish valance spy gels, making the phones
workin the inner spring and sway.

And once I learned ...   woe   the whir
    groom white skinned lion.
                    :Tell me about it, Trawler.

All this before they came   to call me

Bone Breaking Lion   Son of the Buffalo   Cats
   on the Shoulder

I   just a kid.

JANE MUNRO

Blue Sonoma

Somewhere between the directness and clarity of haiku and Yeats's "An aged man is but a paltry thing" moves Jane Munro's hauntingly candid explorations of the hard truths of growing old. But *Blue Sonoma*, unflinching as its poems are in their wrestling with a partner's Alzheimer's, with memory, death, and dying, and with the inexorable advance of time, achieves an engaging liveliness as a result of the poet's earthy voice, colloquial wit, and acute descriptive powers. For Munro, language, travel, and art are the "props / in a little, local theatre of light," and this theatre's relationship to other worlds, other possible states of consciousness, repeatedly leavens *Blue Sonoma*'s painful content with wisdom and delicacy. In primarily short lines of impressive transparency, Munro's writing, replete with natural images of Canada's west coast, celebrates, even as it confronts with blunt honesty, the sensuous passage through the years towards whatever transition must follow. "And us, were we substance or reflection?" The question hovers over this gathering of deeply meditative and viscerally felt poems and leads us, with gentleness but no apology, into the realm of riveting and ultimate contemplation.

Old Man Vacanas

I

The old man
to whom I'm married
hits the sack again
after breakfast.

A black bear
out in the rain
on Blueberry Flats.

Is it too wet
to hibernate? The muddy creek
burgeoning.

By lunch, he's up.
The sky's no lighter – candles
with our tea.

Tell me, can a soul
fatten up for winter?

2

The old man
who works in the garden
grows garlic.

He asks what day it is.
Hail falls.
On every bent leaf, a load
of pearls.
His calendar melts,
its pages slipping into soil.
Bulbs wrap their cloven shoulders
in scraps of tissue paper.

Daffodils
cuffed by squalls
spill scent.
Stout garlic
defends its yard.

None of this matters to him
any more than greying hair.

3

A fire on the hearth, lantern by the bed,
kitchen candelabra in a draft.
Finger of light on an arm of the bench.
One of the cats watching it beckon.

We have met the lion of March.
Today, her tongue abrades my back.

Outside, excuses pile up.
Snow like lamb's wool
sliding down windows.
Posts with stockings about their ankles.

I tuck my hands into my sleeves.
Ravens carry twigs
to their nest in a double-headed cedar.
We who are paired. Even his lips are cold.
Thanks to beams and rafters,
the house becomes a whale.

The miles of intestines facing Jonah.

4

The old man
losing his mind
registers
the weather systems
of intelligence.

Climate change, for all
its extinctions,
won't alter the planet's orbit.

Our laundry tossing,
turning the clearing for a morning
into a ship.

Light billowing through wet sheets.

5

The old man who picks up the phone
does not get your message.

Call again.
Please call again.

The cats leave squirrel guts
on the Tibetan rug.
Augury I cannot read.

You've got to talk with me.

I scrape glistening coils
into a dust pan,
spit on drops of blood and spray ammonia.
The blood spreads into the white wool.

I am so sick of purring beasts.

Don't tempt me, old man.
Today I have four arms
and weapons in each hand.

6

If you want to know the way
out here,
I'll tell you.

Drive and drive.
The road goes up and down, to and fro.

If you want to come visit,
I'll invite you.

My old man won't know
the difference
between you and billy-be-damned.

He's been wearing out old thoughts—
holes now in plenty.
Fewer in his drawers.
And he's not keen on new ones.

We lay the bricks of conversation.
Block one. Block two.
Small. Tidy.
Start again.
Solid. Reassuring.
Four windowless walls.

Roar up the drive. Spit gravel. Blow your horn.

I am gnawing through myself.

7

Doe on the driveway
with this year's fawn
and last year's, now full grown,
eating salmonberry leaves.

Carrying the mail, I walk past.
The deer go on browsing.

My old man
likes magazines. He stands
at the cutting board, leafing through
today's haul. Turns cartoons
in my direction.

Rural postbox half a mile away:
how I keep an eye on the neighbourhood.

Who's laughing at us today?
Fools set in our ways.

8

My old man
oh, my old man, oh my
old man

is lean
as a wooden spoon
stirring batter
that folds
around it the way
at his waist
a softness drapes.

He sleeps on his back,
straight as a broom.
He sleeps on his side,
curled like a cat.
He sleeps with the heater going
and a T-shirt on.
My old man likes
to catch some zzzzzzzs.

9

Now this old man
has ripened sweetly.

He gazes at me,
bemused and happy.

On his way to the sink
he bops the empty coffee pot
on my crown.

The old man
feeding the fire
keeps us primitive.

Dark falling early.
A few sticks in flames
snap their fingers—come,
move your stumps!

The old man pokes at them.
Sparks scatter.

Pull up a chair. Have some wine.
Be our guest.

II

The old man
takes his choppers out
when chicken sticks to them.

He parks them in a glass
of blue fizz.

DNA from fossil bones
tells us we're siblings to Neanderthals—

and the small arrangements
we make? Language, travel, art? Props

in a little, local, theatre of light.

Valley of the Moon

On the drive to the respite hotel,
the *Goldberg Variations*: a bridge to peace.

Sora bidding farewell to Bashō –
Sora leaning forward on his elbow.

*

In the moment of leaving,
when words set sail from paper . . .

soul clings
to one burning
as fire clings to a stick.

*

Even when the mind's a sieve,
soul doesn't grieve –
cannot believe

in scarcity. A mountain,
a river – fully this,
fully that.

RUSSELL THORNTON

The Hundred Lives

The poems in *The Hundred Lives* burn with a rare blend of rhythmic intensity and hard-earned experience that make them at once timeless and contemporary; on page after page, in line after line, we hear the ancient, communal music of language sung through a consciousness of maturity, loss, and restless spiritual hunger. In a very real sense, Thornton's lyric narratives and dialogues — of travel, of Lazarus and the Song of Songs, of romantic love — dramatically enact Robert Frost's notion that the greatest of all attempts is "to say matter in terms of spirit, or spirit in terms of matter, to make the final unity." Thornton speaks with utter conviction and credibility to forge a personal vision, a "pathway through the apple," to an always-richer understanding of human experience. Whether the poems take us to Greece, where gypsy women move "like living tarot in the street," or to the memory of a beloved grandmother "out in the sailing ship of her wedding dress. Her ashes," always *The Hundred Lives* puts us in intimate touch with "first fire, first waters," with the tenderness and pain of vital engagement.

Ouzo

You add water to a glass of ouzo
and a genie-less smoke rises in it asking, "What is it you wish?"
the ardent clear spirit distilled from the lees of wine
suddenly wreathed in opalescent fumes
and boiling away the sediment of your life and distilling the day
while you sit at a rough table in the mid-morning in front of the sea –
so you see there in the glass the vaporous myth of Plato's cave,
the man bound in chains, the theatre of shadows,
and beyond this, the sun's world-filling light.
And the day becomes simpler and simpler,
the day wakes you into light, you drink thick coffee,
walk and swim and sleep in the afternoon,
sit and wait for the blackness of the night to bloom,
the small brilliant white multitudinous flowers of the stars
to bloom from infinitely within the night's blooming.
And there is nothing here to wish for except what is –
nothing except the instant opening,
the sea clear as alcohol, the collapsed waves' foam bubbles
crackling along the sand like a delicate fire,
the distinct self-scoured sand grains, glasses of ouzo themselves,
and the nearby profusion of houses, all exquisite white words
strung around the hills, and the hills a smile of death.
And the old waiter who sets down the ouzo,
who makes his way without effort and with a strange beauty
around and around the perfectly arranged tables,
I see now he is the man who broke free of his chains
and walked out of the cave into the light of day.
It is as if he is the first person I have ever seen;
I do not know how it is that the wrinkles of his face
seem to multiply in the sun, nor how I now look at him through eyes
that are not mine, and he only smiles, for they are his eyes,
nor how it is that he is also young.
His eyes ask me what it is I wish, and he already knows
that it can be nothing except to wait for all blackness to deepen

and become one with all light, the hills here as they darken
and the sun's fire, come into clarity –
to wait for every question to return as an answer;
to wait to be placed in chains endless, transparent,
and travelling the absolute in flow.

Larissa Gypsies

In the out-of-the-way taverna I come to every day,
a Gypsy family is eating an afternoon meal together,
the moustached father not looking up from his beans and bread,
the trio of shoeless children, all girls, preening themselves,
the young, worn mother looking away intently yet unfixedly.
Two passersby, other Gypsy women, stop,
turn their heads and launch an insult in across the handful of tables.
The young mother launches back an apparently inspired response
and instantly the exchange escalates into a full-blown verbal brawl.
The women outside begin shouting, spitting and making obscene
     gestures.
The woman inside begins shouting, spitting and making obscene
     gestures.
The taverna customers, the dozen or so of them, keep quiet,
until after some minutes a young man sniggers uneasily,
then another slips a glance at the taverna owner.
Suddenly, the taverna owner, fed up, marches up to the Gypsies'
     table
and orders, "Get out! Get out! Don't ever come back!"
The woman, however, is not paying him the least bit of attention.
Her husband, expressionless, is calmly eating,
her children are calmly putting the last of their food into their
     mouths.
Now the taverna owner, grabbing the woman, tries to remove her
     from her chair.
"All right, all right," she ends up relenting, "I'm going, I'm going,"
and finally stands up and walks out, husband and children in tow.
And now most of the taverna customers have stopped eating
and become an audience for the afternoon spectacle.
The taverna owner is out on the sidewalk shooing the Gypsies away,
while the three Gypsy women continue arguing, dancing around
     each other
and uttering forth a concoction of Greek, Turkish and Romany.

Even the Greeks, who have known Gypsy people all their lives,
    are awestruck.
These women, awkward and uncouth at the world's table –
they are the unbroken ones, never to be corralled,
fierce, free and playful out there in the air glistening as with their
    own gazes,
they are like winds from a wildly loved nowhere, laden with savage
    roses,
they are like living tarot scattered in the street.

Turning the Lamb

It was my turn to sit and rotate the handle of the spit.
The whole lamb had been roasting since morning,
now it was glistening, juices trickling steadily out of it.
The lamb fumes thickened. I sat inches away
from the bed of coals, the heat in my face,
the brilliant white light of the Greek spring in my eyes,
looking out at you, your mother, your aunts, uncles, cousins.
Music had been put on, and was pulsing and blaring
into the walled space out back of your apartment,
and you and the other young women among your relatives
all took hands and began doing traditional dances.
As you went around and around, and back and forth,
you smiled and never let your eyes leave mine.
That was when your mother saw we were together
and called you a whore out of her eyes. And I thought
of her father the surgeon and Greek resistance fighter
starved to death in a blocked cave, of her husband
returning to his girlfriend a few weeks after her wedding,
and of the photo in her bedroom of you in her arms
when you were a baby. She would now do everything
she could to make me stay here, or to keep us a secret
while working at forcing me to leave. The day
continued, the lamb crackling, the music blaring,
moments reaching pitches of wild, uncanny joy
and boundlessness, moments immediately circumscribed,
quieted within the charged yet calm flow
in the circle of clasped hands. I took my turn
again, again. Everyone was drunk on Amstel beer
or village wine and half full on platters of french fries.
Finally it was time to gorge on the Easter Day meal.
One of the cousins sliced and piled on platters
unimaginably succulent pieces of the young lamb
to be circulated, and I sat and did not refuse to eat and eat.
Slowly the older ones headed into the apartment.

The younger ones, dazed and sleepy, followed.
All lay down in beds and on couches. I lay down in turn,
as I had sat to attend to the lamb. After a few hours
it was evening, and people rose and ate and drank again.
The music sounded different now, and I could understand
the Greek words and how the singer was drowning
and wanted to be thrown farther out to sea, was burning
and wanted more oil to be poured onto the fire.
The dancing resumed, the music grew loud and swerved
as the singer became more and more ecstatic, and I saw myself
still sitting near the lamb on its spit, as at a strict interface,
and shouted and pleaded within, slaughterer and slaughtered.

Letters

I threw away your letters.
Years ago, just like that.
The tight black swirls,
circles and strokes
filling fine sheets —
I would not see them again.
The last items I had left.
The dates. The phrases.
The things you said. Forfeited.
Snowflake patterns.
Leaf diagrams.
Crushed. Melted. Dissolved.
The flooding runoff
at the backed-up
street corner drain
collects it all.
Only the opening
of a strong seal far below
could allow that pool
of darkening rainwater
to run and drop away
between the slats.
If I were to recover
the lost key of the cursive,
I would in one instant
want back again what I saw
in the images
the hand traced out for me.
And would be denied
even the little
the letters kept of you
and be released
into nothing but more time.

Anniversaries, End of August

Anniversaries circle round again. My grandparents
marrying in the sun. The guests in their best attire.
The filled vaulted room. Then the clinking glasses.
Then the private rites of those who waited long.
It is there in the light. Light that is a window.
And is a mirroring sea for my grandmother
out in the sailing ship of her wedding dress. Her ashes.

Someone I loved dying alone. The month the wide frame
of her final leaving. It was also her birth month. Light
opens its window, and is window upon window.
Her living hair darkens beyond its living black.
That black is another light, no visible sun
burning in its origins but a dark transparency,
and it arrives like another her, again and again.

I too am a window. In August, two people
among the dead look out of it. They do not know
the window is me. And I am what a window can wish.
To open endlessly because it is light,
and because it is a mirror, let the silver erase itself
and arrive and wait flawless on the glass,
and darken, and erase itself, like life, like death.

A List

Once, I would make certain my name
did not appear in any directory. Now
I dream I am back in different times and places,
and the people I remember I loved
are not there, and the places not at all
as they were, and it is as if I have belonged
to some underground organization
set up to allow no member
to betray another – no member ever
knowing who his associates actually are.

Now I agree to be listed, I ask to be listed –
and hope that this will make it easy to find me.
And now I dream of a list. On it
everything I and those I have been with
have ever truly felt or done is recorded
in the clearest detail. In the same dream
is a man who walks alongside me and knows
nothing but the entire list by heart,
and will recite it to the moment I die,
and then he too will disappear.

THE POETS

SHANE BOOK is an award-winning poet and filmmaker. He was educated at the University of Victoria, the Iowa Writers' Workshop, and Stanford University, where he was a Wallace Stegner Fellow. His writing has appeared in more than twenty anthologies, including *The Great Black North: Contemporary African Canadian Poetry*.

ELEANOR GOODMAN is a writer and translator. She is a Research Associate at the Fairbank Center at Harvard University and spent a year at Peking University on a Fulbright Fellowship. Her book of translations, *Something Crosses My Mind*, by Wang Xiaoni was the recipient of a 2013 PEN/Heim Translation Grant. Goodman has been an artist in residence at the American Academy in Rome, was awarded a Henry Luce Translation Fellowship from the Vermont Studio Center, and received the International Merit Award in Poetry from the *Atlanta Review*. Her work appears in publications such as *PN Review, The Quarterly Conversation, Fiction, Pathlight, Cha, The Guardian, Pleiades, Acumen, Perihelion, The Los Angeles Review,* and on *The Best American Poetry* web site.

WIOLETTA GREG is a poet, writer, editor, and translator. Born in southern Poland, she moved to the UK in 2006 and currently resides in the town of Ryde on the Isle of Wight. Greg has published several volumes of poetry in Poland, Canada, and the UK, including *Wyobraźnia kontrolowana* (*Controlled Imagination*, 1988); *Parantele* (*Kinships*, 2003); *Orinoko* (2008); *Inne obroty* (*Alternate Turns*, 2010); the bilingual *Pamięć Smieny/Smena's Memory* (2011);

the collection of short prose forms *Notatnik z wyspy* (*Notes from an Island*, 2011); and a debut novel, *Guguly* (2014) in which she revisits the experience of growing up in Communist Poland. Her poems have appeared in numerous literary journals and she has won several literary prizes, including the Tyska Zima Poetycka.

MAREK KAZMIERSKI is a writer, publisher, and translator. He escaped communist Poland as a child and settled in the UK. Joint winner of the Decibel Penguin Prize and sole recipient of the *BIKE Magazine* Philosopher of the Year award, Marek is also the managing editor of a prison literary magazine, *Not Shut Up*, and founder of OFF_PRESS, an independent publishing house which has worked with English PEN, the South Bank Centre, the Polish Cultural Institute, the Mayor of London, and various universities across Europe. His work has been published in numerous journals and titles, including *The Guardian, 3AM Magazine*, and *Poetry Wales*. This book was translated during his residency at Villa Decius in Krakow, Poland, courtesy of The Polish Book Institute.

MICHAEL LONGLEY was born in Belfast in 1939. He has published nine collections of poetry including *Gorse Fires* (1991), which won the Whitbread Poetry Award, and *The Weather in Japan* (2000), which won the Hawthornden Prize, the T.S. Eliot Prize, and the *Irish Times* Poetry Prize. In 2001 he received the Queen's Gold Medal for Poetry and in 2003 the Wilfred Owen Award. He was awarded a CBE in 2010 and was Ireland Professor of Poetry, 2007–2010.

JANE MUNRO is the author of five previous books of poetry, most recently *Active Pass* (2010) and *Point No Point* (2006). Her work has received the Bliss Carman Poetry Award, the Macmillan Prize for Poetry, and been nominated for the Pat Lowther Award. She is a member of Yoko's Dogs (Jan Conn, Mary di Michele, Susan Gillis, Jane Munro), a poetry collective whose first book *Whisk* was published in 2013. After living for twenty years on the southwest coast of Vancouver Island, she has now returned to Vancouver.

SPENCER REECE is a poet and priest. His first collection, *The Clerk's Tale*, won the Bakeless Prize in 2003. He has received an NEA grant, a Guggenheim grant, a Witter Bynner Prize from the Library of Congress, a Whiting Writers' Award, and the Amy Lowell Traveling Scholarship. His poems have been published in *The New Yorker*, *Poetry*, *The American Scholar*, and *The New Republic*. He served at the Honduran orphanage, Our Little Roses, and works for the Bishop of Spain for the Reformed Episcopal Church, Iglesia Española Reformada Episcopal.

RUSSELL THORNTON has published five previous books of poetry, with *House Built of Rain* being shortlisted for the BC Book Prize and the ReLit Poetry Award and *Birds, Metals, Stones & Rain* shortlisted for the 2013 Governor General's Award. Thornton won the League of Canadian Poets National Contest in 2000 and *The Fiddlehead* magazine's Ralph Gustafson Prize in 2009. He lives in North Vancouver.

WANG XIAONI was born in Changchun, Jilin, near the border with North Korea, in 1955 and spent seven years as a labourer in the countryside during the Cultural Revolution. In 1977 she was accepted into the Chinese Department at Jilin University and in 1985 she moved to Shenzhen, in southern China. She is one of the few women associated with the "Misty" poets, though her poetry tends to focus on what she calls "the complex state of the human psyche" and avoids the overtly political. Wang has worked as a film script editor and college professor. Her publications include more than twenty-five books of poetry, essays, and novels.

THE JUDGES

TIM BOWLING is the author of twelve poetry collections, including *Selected Poems* (2013) and *Circa Nineteen Hundred and Grief* (2014) and of four novels and two works of non-fiction. His work has received a Guggenheim Fellowship, two nominations for the Governor General's Literary Award, two Writers' Trust nominations, and five Alberta Book Awards. Originally from Ladner, British Columbia, he now resides in Edmonton, Alberta.

FANNY HOWE has written numerous books of fiction. Howe's collections of poetry include *Second Childhood* (2014), *Come and See* (2011), *On the Ground* (2004), *Gone* (2003), *Selected Poems* (2000), *Forged* (1999), *Q* (1998), *One Crossed Out* (1997), *O'Clock* (1995), and *The End* (1992). She has won a Guggenheim Fellowship and the Ruth Lilly Lifetime Achievement Award, among others. She lives in Massachusetts and is currently a Visiting Writer at Brown University.

PIOTR SOMMER has written numerous books in Polish and is the author of twelve books of poetry, including *Dni i noce* (2009, *Days and Nights*) and *Wiersze ze słów* (2009, *Poems from Words*), and a selected poems, *Po ciemku tez* (2013). He has published an anthology of contemporary British poetry, and a book of interviews with British and Irish poets. He has translated Robert Lowell into Polish and produced Polish editions of Frank O'Hara and Charles Reznikoff. His books in English are *Things to Translate* (1991), *Continued* (2005), and *Overdoing It* (2013). He has taught at several American universities, was visiting translator at Warwick University in England, and has been awarded numerous prizes, including the Selesius Poetry Prize (2010). He is a freelance writer, editor, and translator and lives outside of Warsaw, Poland.

ACKNOWLEDGEMENTS

The publisher thanks the following for their kind permission to reprint the work contained in this volume:

"The Watermelon's Sorrow," "Seeing the Ocean from a Night Flight," "Plowman," "Wheat Seedlings," "At the Village Fair," "At Night What's Inside the Skyscrapers," and "The One Sticking Close to the White Wall as He Leaves" from *Something Crosses My Mind* by Wang Xiaoni, translated by Eleanor Goodman, are reprinted by permission of Zephyr Press.

"Half-Term," "Smena's Memory," "Spring, 1986," "Stargate," "Pips," and "A Wedding Party" from *Finite Formulae & Theories of Chance* by Wioletta Greg, translated by Marek Kazmierski are reprinted by permission of Arc Publications.

"The Stairwell," "Notebook," "Amelia's Poem," "Marigolds, 1960," "Boat," "Psalm," "Hailstones," "The Wheelchair," and "The Mule-Cart" from *The Stairwell* by Michael Longley are reprinted by permission of Jonathan Cape.

"1 Corinthians 13," "The Prodigal Son," "A Few Tender Minutes," and "The Poor" from *The Road to Emmaus* by Spencer Reece are reprinted by permission of Farrar, Straus and Giroux.

"Old Man Vacanas," and "Valley of the Moon" from *Blue Sonoma* by Jane Munro are reprinted by permission of Brick Books.

THE GRIFFIN POETRY PRIZE
Anthology 2015

The best books of poetry published in English internationally and in Canada are honoured each year with the $65,000 Griffin Poetry Prize, one of the world's most prestigious and valuable literary awards. Since 2001 this annual prize has acted as a tremendous spur to interest in and recognition of poetry, focusing worldwide attention on the formidable talent of poets writing in English. Each year the editor of *The Griffin Poetry Prize Anthology* gathers the work of the extraordinary poets shortlisted for the awards and introduces us to some of the finest poems in their collections.

This year, editor and prize juror Tim Bowling's selections from the international shortlist include poems from Wang Xiaoni's *Something Crosses My Mind* (Zephyr Press), translated by Eleanor Goodman, Wioletta Greg's *Finite Formulae & Theories of Chance* (Arc Publications), translated by Marek Kazmierski, Michael Longley's *The Stairwell* (Jonathan Cape), and Spencer Reece's *The Road to Emmaus* (Farrar, Straus and Giroux). The selections from the Canadian shortlist include poems from Shane Book's *Congotronic* (House of Anansi), Jane Munro's *Blue Sonoma* (Brick Books), and Russell Thornton's *The Hundred Lives* (Quattro Books).

In choosing the 2015 shortlist, prize jurors Tim Bowling, Fanny Howe, and Piotr Sommer each read 560 books of poetry, from 42 countries, including 24 translations. The jury also wrote the citations that introduce the seven poets' nominated works. Royalties generated from *The Griffin Poetry Prize Anthology 2015* will be donated to UNESCO's World Poetry Day, which was created to support linguistic diversity through poetic expression and to offer endangered languages the opportunity to be heard in their communities.

The Griffin Trust

Mark Doty
Carolyn Forché
Scott Griffin
Michael Ondaatje
Robin Robertson
Karen Solie
Colm Tóibín
David Young

Trustees Emeritus

Margaret Atwood
Robert Hass